The Voice of Fai

Valley of Achor

Vol. 2

Being a series of letters to several friends on religious subjects

J. Church

Alpha Editions

This edition published in 2024

ISBN : 9789362991782

Design and Setting By
Alpha Editions
www.alphaedis.com
Email - info@alphaedis.com

As per information held with us this book is in Public Domain.
This book is a reproduction of an important historical work. Alpha Editions uses the best technology to reproduce historical work in the same manner it was first published to preserve its original nature. Any marks or number seen are left intentionally to preserve its true form.

Contents

LETTER I. .... - 1 -
LETTER II. .... - 2 -
LETTER III. .... - 3 -
LETTER IV. .... - 4 -
LETTER V. .... - 5 -
LETTER VI. .... - 6 -
LETTER VII. .... - 7 -
LETTER VIII. .... - 9 -
LETTER IX. .... - 11 -
LETTER X. .... - 13 -
LETTER XI. .... - 16 -
LETTER XII. .... - 19 -
LETTER XIII. .... - 21 -
LETTER XIV .... - 23 -
LETTER XV. .... - 26 -
LETTER XVI. .... - 28 -
LETTER XVII. .... - 30 -
LETTER XVIII. .... - 32 -

LETTER I.

Valley of Achor, June 1, 1819.

Dear Mr. HAIRBY,

I have sent you a little more scribble to read, which will amuse you for an hour. Will you be so kind as to send them all to Mrs. HARRIS? You need not seal them, though I hope the Lord will seal you; but he has already, for the spirit in the heart is the king's seal, saying, *This* is mine—the Church is a fountain sealed; and every sensible token that you have had, every smile and ray of spiritual joy, every gracious promise applied to the heart, and every time love is sensibly felt, this is the sealing of the Spirit. Christ was sealed by the Father when he was chosen in eternity, he was the Son of God; but perhaps he was not sensibly sealed by the Holy Spirit till his baptism, when, probably, both the Father and the Holy Spirit spoke, This is my beloved Son, *in* whom I am well pleased. This is my beloved Son, *with* whom I am well pleased. So says St. Matthew and St. Mark. God has chosen us in Christ, this is the Father's sealing; but the Holy Spirit in us, is the Spirit's seal, and every gracious look, intercourse, and holy frame, is the sealing work. This is not faith, but it is the enjoyment of the object we do believe in. Faith is a radical principle, and always abides in the heart: But after ye believed ye were sealed by the Holy Spirit of Promise. This sealing is the sensible enjoyment of the promised good. I beg dear Mrs. H— to notice this. A little sacred comfort arising from believing, hoping, and trusting in the finished work of Christ, is also the sealing work; and, perhaps, in the closing scene of life, when she draws near to death, this will be more blessedly enjoyed—For my people shall be satisfied with my goodness saith the Lord.

Your's,
Ruhamah.

LETTER II.

Valley of Achor, August 10, 1819.

To THE SAME.

MY DEAR SIR,

How gracious is the Lord: when I cannot believe, still *he* abideth faithful—Oh! for an heart to love him, and to adore him; but though I have often rebelled, yet, how gracious and faithful he still continues towards me—surely faithfulness is the girdle of his reins. This is the girdle for faith to lay hold of. My faith has only to do with his promises, the *whens*, the *wheres*, and the *hows*; this is the Lord's work, and not mine. I wish above all things for an increase of faith, of hope, and love; the sweetest is love: but though I have so sweetly felt this lately, it is now suspended, yet I hope it will return. I am now in my old place, a poor, vile, guilty creature, at the feet of Jesus, pleading his work again; and looking now, *not* at what I feel, but at the satisfaction of Christ, with which the Father is everlastingly well pleased. Here I rest, till love is felt again; my desire is to him, and to the remembrance of his name. Sin works, Satan is busy, but grace still reigns. Thus we see that grace has yet the honor of the field. We have not run back, though we have often been down, the Lord raises us up again, and this motto is our privilege, "I shall arise." Oh! what a mercy, greater is he that is in us, than he that is in the world. I have cause to be thankful to the Lord that he has thus far led me; but the Devil, at times, almost drives me distracted with the carking cares of what will happen to me. Oh! lay my case before God, that I may have power to cast this burthen on the Lord. I wish I could get over it; yet my fears may be a good sign, better fear than to presume, or grow careless.

Love to Mrs. H. and Daughter,
Ruhamah.

LETTER III.

Valley of Achor, Jan. 10, 1819

To THE SAME.

DEAR SIR,

I hope you are all well in health. I have been poorly in body and mind, but have been supported; *his* left hand I found was under my head, but I wanted his right hand to embrace me; the one is daily manifested, and the other is always wanted, though but seldom felt. Yet he has embraced us, and Solomon says, there is a time to embrace, and there is a time to refrain from embracing. Christ received us to the glory of God in the eternal covenant. The Father draws us to Christ, by giving us to feel our sinful state, our weakness and wants; and then by setting before us his dear Son in his ability and willingness to save. In his light we see him, desire him, move in heart after him, and long for a smile of his approbation—to feel it, and enjoy it, knowing that eternal life is in it. These workings of the mind are often attended with fears, bondage, doubts, and misgivings, and these rise as hope gets down; but as faith gathers strength, so we rise above these doubts. This has been my experience for many years, and I have now a good opportunity of watching it. Some, indeed, get to land upon the broad planks of the promises, and sensible manifestations of divine love; but myself, and many more, will arrive as safe home, only by getting hold of a few scattered truths, which we love and embrace. Receive the truth, and the truth shall make you free. And one truth is—I have blotted out as a thick cloud thy sins.—We are all much tried, but it is our appointed lot—discouraged because of the way. And are these the blessings we expect? Is this the lot of God's elect? Yes; this lot is cast into the lap, but the whole disposing is of the Lord.—Let this note be read to dear Mrs. H. Grace be with you all.

So prays,
Ruhamah.

LETTER IV.

Valley of Achor, May 21, 1819.

To THE SAME.

DEAR SIR,

When you have read these letters, be so kind as to send one to the Post Office, and the other, if you could call on Mrs. L—, she would take it kind, as she is indisposed. She was confined many weeks, and no one in the Church knew it, or else they would have visited her. I wish I was able, but even then I should feel no desire, except the Lord gave it me. When we are in bondage of spirit, the heart is contracted, and we can feel for no one but ourselves; but when love operates, and keeps the heart open, we can then sympathize with the Lord's afflicted ones; our hearts are enlarged to them, to their Lord, and to the truth as it is in Jesus. As these sweet sensations of love are felt, we melt and mourn. These are the sweetest moments of my life, and many such I have had these three weeks past. These cause me songs in the house of my pilgrimage, yet I cannot sing, I can only look on, and wonder, while the Angel does marvellously before me. I am but low in body, and a sweet lowness of mind, and here I am most safe: I beg for the increase of it, but I am fearful of losing it, knowing that the Son of Man is at times taken away: then do we fast in those days. But we are getting home—happy meeting by and by—

> There may I meet my sincere friends,
>   Amidst the ransom'd throng;
> Where love and friendship have no end,
>   And you will join the song.

Love to Mrs. H. and Children—excuse haste.

Your's,
Ruhamah.

LETTER V.

Valley of Achor, April 12, 1819.

To the SAME.

MY DEAR SIR,

I hope your faith is fixed upon, and growing into, a most divine acquaintance with the *three* grand Favors the gospel holds out to you; each adorable Person in the ever adorable Trinity, proclaiming, I am thy God: and this Favor seen through a fourth, even the human nature of Christ; while pardon, justification, and the gift of the Holy Spirit, also shine through the word in your mind: these also producing love, wonder, and praise; and these opposed by the world, the flesh, and the devil, often stirring up fear, rebellion, and ingratitude, till we are favored again with fresh power, fresh views, and fresh strength; encouraging and confirming faith, hope, and patience, and working in prayer, hearing, and reading, till we find it sweet to talk, meditate, and praise. Soon we shall see three wonders; Christ in person, the angels in light, and the glorified Church of the redeemed in full dress. We are in our dishabille at present; the world knoweth us not, because it doth not yet appear what we shall be; but we shall be like *him*, as sure as we love him now. Do tell Mrs. H. this glory is for them that wait for him, them that trust in him, and them who love his various visits; and I am sure this will encourage her. Mark it: *those who hope in his mercy*; and that mercy is Christ.

Your's, truly,
Ruhamah.

LETTER VI.

Valley of Achor, Dec. 19, 1817.

Dear Mr. E.

When the dear apostles of old wrote their epistles to the churches, after having stated the glory and preciousness of Christ, they generally mentioned some name of the adorable Father, as suited to that Church to whom they wrote. When Peter addressed the churches scattered abroad, during the persecution under the pagan emperors, he mentioned the glorious character of God, as the God of all grace—*all* grace which they could need.—Paul mentions to one church, the God of hope; to another, the God of patience, and the God of all consolation. These titles are exceedingly precious; and as they are suited to the churches of old, they are handed down to us, as they suit us now; and indeed whatever precious character the Lord bears, it is in mercy to us—these are not empty titles, but very important parts of that work, undertaken by the adorable Trinity ere time began. It is surprising grace that God should ever go forth in creature acts of love to us—that he should pass by others—that he should occupy his thoughts about us, who are but mere worms, clods of earth. This is wonderful, that he should love us, though fallen, polluted, distant, and awfully rebellious—that he should ever visit, abide, and dwell with us: this is surprising grace, stupendous mercy indeed, that the Lord should ever send a promise to the heart, and make that promise good to such unbelieving, unworthy beings. These things will, no doubt, astonish the saints of God in glory for ever. O, that they had better effect upon our hearts! and the reason why they have not, is owing to the weakness of our faith; and faith is weakened as the word of God, the throne of God, and the people of God are neglected. As sin is winked at, and lies upon the mind almost unseen, and, of course, unlamented—this weakens precious faith. May the Lord keep up those two useful agents in our souls, *Watchful* and *All-prayer*.

With respect to myself, I am kept passive in my Lord's hands. I sensibly feel my situation; I am certainly very low, but I have many mercies. My faith and confidence increases in the Lord's designs, at least, in the *end* designed; and when I am tried *enough*, I shall come forth as gold. Jesus is a refiner and purifyer; his dear people are compared to gold and silver—if they were only wooden vessels, they would be burnt with the fire of tribulation; but then, though they cannot be consumed, the apostle intimates their works—some hay, straw, and stubble—must be burnt, though himself shall be saved, yet so as by fire.

Your's, truly,
Ruhamah.

LETTER VII.

Achor's Vale, June 14, 1819.

Mrs. E.

MY DEAR FRIEND,

I trust you are better in health than you was; I feel very anxious about you both; I pray God to spare you, to see his good hand of grace toward me; and that he has heard many prayers on my behalf, although he has not heard them in the way I requested; but though the Lord often changes his promise, yet, he never breaks his promise. He often changes the promise of a temporal blessing into a spiritual good; but he never changes his mind nor falsifies his word—he is the only faithful Friend on whom we can rely; all others are like glasses, they are to be used, but no weight to be put upon them. Hence the command, Trust ye not in a friend; lean not too heavy, nor build upon glass. This blessing is the gift of God, it is grace given to the friend; and it is worthy of observation, that a disposition to act friendly, is from God, and the befriended should look to Jesus through the friend, as Christ shines through them. And this is evidenced by the effects produced, because it draws up the mind to the Saviour in a way of gratitude and wonder, love and praise. I will magnify the Lord with a song. The shall please the Lord better than a bullock that hath horns and hoofs. This is the way the Lord deals, at times, with me; when particularly sensible of sin, I confess, supplicate, plead, and submit; if grief overflow, I pray, read much, and think; and when I am favored with the least glimpse of his face, or a sensation of his love, or a little life in my spirit, then I praise, love, adore, and offer up the sacrifice of thanksgiving—this is called the calves of the lips.

I have not written my thoughts on the subject we last discoursed on, but shall by and by, God willing. I have been much grieved lately that Mr. — has made use of such warm expressions in the pulpit, concerning the decrees of God. What he has asserted are undoubted truths, but I object to the *manner* in which they are stated. I have no objection to the preaching these awful and sublime subjects, but it requires a man of *some* wisdom to state them properly, or else the subject may be rendered disgustful, even to believers themselves. God has chosen his people in Christ before the world began: this is a truth worthy of our deepest regard; that the Lord should cause millions and millions of beings, angels and men, to rise in his infinite mind, and out of them to select a people for himself, to the glory of his own name, and, as a Sovereign, to display upon them the riches of his grace—this was the favour shewed them, and this favour is called *grace*, electing sovereign grace, because he passed the rest by, he did not confer on them this favour. No reason can be assigned for this, but his own sovereign goodwill. The rest he passed by; he did not choose them to damn them, nor predestinate them to be damned, nor make them on purpose to damn them; that was not the business; he passed them by in reference to his act, but he chose the rest, both angels and men, in the dear Covenant Head, and fixed them, standing most secure in Christ, before they fell. Those whom the Lord passed by, stood in Adam only; here they sinned, fell, and became guilty: as they grow up, they evidence God has passed them by, as they live and die regardless of God, ignorant of the Saviour, and heart enemies to him; but as God did not choose the elect for any foreseen good in them, or done by them, so neither did he pass by the rest because they would be so vile, but he chose the one in the riches of his grace, and passed by the other in his divine sovereignty. Mark—he does not damn them because he is a Sovereign, and has a right to do it; No, he only passed by them as a Sovereign, and he punishes them because they hate him, and have so awfully signed against him, so that our God is holy, gracious, sovereign, and just.

I thought it acceptable to you, to drop you this line, to state the simple truth as it is in scripture; a subject that puzzled me for many years, and which has still a mystery in it that we cannot comprehend; yet there is enough revealed to faith to receive, admire, and adore. And as to the damnation of infants, which Mr. — advanced last Sunday, the scriptures are silent about it; nor do I think it forms any part of the gospel which Jesus and Paul preached. We have nothing to do with it. Where the bible has no mouth, we ought to have no ears. I am of opinion that children are saved, but I have no positive scripture for it—as the glories of heaven are rather described by negatives, what they are not, so the salvation of children is by a negative also, where they are not; for in the account of those that are lost, and in hell now, and will be punished there, we read nothing of children. Our dear friend Mr. Fosset, wishes me to write on these subjects, at the next church meeting, to set this matter at rest a little, by explaining the subject in my simple, humble manner. What a mercy the Lord has not passed us by, as he might have done; and as an evidence he loves us, he has given us some taste of that love, and created his fear in our hearts.

Your's
Ruhamah.

LETTER VIII.

Valley of Achor, Sept. 15, 1818.

MY DEAR FRIEND, Mr. C.

I thank you kindly for the loan of books. I return you the Pamphlet written by Mr. Gadsby. I quite agree with him in his views of the Moral Law, which is commonly termed so, but which the Apostle stiles *spiritual*. I consider the Gospel of the grace of God, the Father's will to us, in Christ Jesus, containing *Promises, Declarations of Mercy, Imitations, Precepts, and Exhortations*, to be the only, and all-sufficient Rule of a Christian. These are not in opposition to the holy Law of God, but they far excel it in glory, and as many as walk according to this Rule, peace be on them. Christ is our King and our Lawgiver, he has fulfilled the Law for his Church, brought in an everlasting righteousness for our justification; he has put away sin by the sacrifice of himself, and he lives a life of mediation for all who come to God through him. The Holy Spirit illuminates the mind; reveals pardon to the conscience; and sheds abroad the love of God in the heart, plants his fear in the soul, and enables us to take the will of God for our Rule, as it is expressed in the Gospel.—This is our rule of walk, conduct, and conversation—the Lord help us to walk in this light, as God is in the light. But I think it is cruel for any Preacher or Author, who professes to be a leader of God's people, to send them to the Law, in *any sense whatever*. Every worldling and proud Pharisee should be sent there, till they are taught their need of Christ. But an humble, regenerate person, should always be directed to the Lord Jesus, to the throne of grace, and to the glorious Gospel of grace. None but worldly Wisemen will ever direct either a burthened Pilgrim, or a consistent believer, to the Law. John Bunyan met with such a director, but what his feelings were he tells you: First, he forsook the advice: of the Gospel Minister, *Evangelist*, who gave him this direction, *Look unto Jesus*. Secondly, He tried to raise a prejudice in his mind against the Ministers who preach free grace. Thirdly, He directed him to go by the high hill that he pointed to. This is the way that seemeth right to a man, but it is falling from grace: the spirit of bondage began to work on his mind; his fears of the curse of this broken Covenant increased; his guilt was deeper felt, because he was out of the way. A sense of God's anger flashed on his spirit, and the dread of damnation overcame him. He quaked for fear. This is coming to Mount Sinai indeed, and this is all the Law can do, viz. Convince and condemn—and these feelings, more or less, attend those who are seeking to the Law for life, hope, peace, and salvation; or that cleave to it in *any sense whatever:* for what things soever the law saith, it saith to them that are under it, whether they are in a profession or out of it; and as many as are of the works of the law, are under the curse of it—but we are redeemed from that broken covenant, that we should serve the Lord Jesus in the newness of the spirit, and not in the oldness of the letter. But do read what Evangelist says of such Law Preachers, and Directors, in his conversation with the Pilgrim, when he met him near Mr. Legality's House.

May you and I walk in Christ, die to sin, and live more to God.—Kind respects to Mrs. C. and Brother.

Your's,
Ruhamah.

LETTER IX.

Achor's Vale, May 6, 1819.

MY DEAR FRIEND, Miss BRAES,

History relates a poor aged man, who had once been serviceable to his country, and was condemned by a Tyrant to be starved to death in prison. All were astonished that he did not die, seeing no food was brought to him; but it was found afterwards that his married daughter visited him twice a day, and gave him suck from her own breast. This is an instance of filial affection. You have acted almost as kind, in its degree, to me; and with your dear aunt, you have often soothed my sorrows with the milk of human kindness. May my Lord reward it another day. You have heard my poor feeble sermons with pleasure, especially when I have been enabled to point out the beauties, and glories of the *Friend* of guilty man. I hope I am only learning better how to extol and magnify the grace, the love, the person, and work of *him*, who, to a grace-taught eye, is fairer than the children of men. I have, indeed, fell into a place where two seas meet—the malice of Satan and the power of man; yet, through grace, and when it is well with me, I have this confidence, *I shall arise*; but how, and when, I leave it with God. I am at times troubled about it, but at other times I can cast that burden on the Lord. I wish it laid in my power to write something to you of the dear Saviour, that would lead you to admire and adore him. I have said a little about him, but, alas, it was little indeed. He is the bright Sun in the firmament of heaven, all the millions of angels and spirits of just men who are now in glory, look upon him with wonder and delight; and while they gaze, he fills them with joy, with peace, with love, and with the most solid satisfaction. They wondered at his love when on earth, that he should ever bleed and agonize, sigh and die for them; but, what must they think now they see him in his full glory?

> And *now* they range the heavenly plains,
> And sing *his* love in sweetest strains;
> Or, overwhelm'd with rapture sweet,
> Sink down, adoring at his feet.

Because *he* is so glorious, so beautiful, so lovely, and so kind. He saw what poor guilty creatures we should be, condemned to eternal misery and woe. *He* knew we could not help ourselves out of this state. *He* knew God was just in condemning us, and he knew that God, as an unchangeable Being, could not alter his oath, As I live, the soul that sinneth shall die! We had broken his Law; we were born in sin; we went astray from infancy, and must have strayed into everlasting darkness, but,

> With pitying eye the Prince of Peace,
> Beheld our helpless grief.

He took our nature, engaged to fulfil the Law we had broken, and pay the dreadful debt of suffering. This *he* did heartily for us, and is now in glory, pleading the virtue of that work, and receiving all that come to God by *him*.

Sing, oh ye heavens, Jesus hath done it, and done it, I trust, for my dear young Friend, to whom I write with pleasure. Need I say to you that you stand in need of this Saviour? I hope you are in a little measure convinced of it, and at times, when no eye can see you but the Saviour's, you send up many an humble wish, fervent desires, and earnest breathings, that the ever-blessed Spirit would teach you Christ, and shew you that your sins are pardoned, that your interest is sure, and that the dear Lord thought upon *you* when *he* engaged to die for sinners—that *he* thought upon you when he entered into the garden of sorrow, and when *he* said, It is finished! Do often, secretly lift up your heart to *him*, saying, Lord shew me that thou lovest me. This is done by the Spirit and by the Word. May *he* be very precious to you; and do remember *he* hath said, They that seek *me* shall find me. Blessed is she that believeth, for there shall be a performance of those things that are told her from the Lord.

And now do accept my sincerest thanks for your affectionate kindness.

Your's,
Ruhamah.

LETTER X.

Valley of Achor, May 16, 1819.

MY DEAR FRIEND, Mrs. HARRIS,

I am sorry to hear of your indisposition, but hope also to hear soon of your recovery. I take this opportunity of acknowledging how much I feel indebted to you for your long concern for my best interest, and your grief for my trials; but I think God has given you many tokens of my future good, by many gracious impressions on your mind in your sleeping hours, and I trust we shall not be mistaken in them, although we are apt to construe such impressions to mere temporal advantages, just as the Apostles did of our dear Lord's kingdom and government; they all thought he was come to set up a temporal kingdom, but when they were filled with the Holy Spirit they understood the subject better. This world is not our rest, we are not born merely to pass our lives in this, but to be looking out for a better and more enduring home: yet, alas, how prone are we to fix our tents here, in this world of uncertainty and trouble. I trust my dear friend has a little hope of a better world. You have often heard of an eternal glory, and I am sure it will be a heaven worth dying for. Many of the people of the world rush into wars and bloodshed, the ruins of countries and the distress of nations, merely to get a great name, and that it might be said they died honorably in the field of battle. Poor deluded creatures, this was not worth dying for; honour and fame is but a noise, a vapour, a puff, and a breath. But we want to die to obtain a glorious eternity, to see the dear Saviour, to be with him, and to be like him; to see him with our enlightened understandings, till the last trumpet shall sound, and our bodies be raised from the dead, strong, beautiful, and glorious, and the soul and body meet again with rapture, to be filled with the joy of the Lord, to hear the welcome sentence of the dear Redeemer, and see him smile on us, creating our heaven, and delighting us with his love; opening our minds to receive the knowledge of God in his glorious persons, the greatness of his grace, the displays of his wisdom and power—his truth, condescension, faithfulness, and mercy in our eternal salvation.

I trust my dear kind Friend can say she humbly desires only Christ and an interest in him, to know that her sins are pardoned by him, and that she lives in the tenderest affections of his heart. The scriptures declare that you do live there, but you want to feel it for yourself; yet, I hope you can say, from what little you do know, you depend upon Christ as God-Man and Mediator, upon his most blessed work, as your acceptance with the Father, only you want the gracious Holy Spirit to shew you so much of Christ as to cause you to love *him* above all things, and to give you the clearest assurance of his love to you. *Do take notice.* This little knowledge you have of *him*, and this desire after *him*, this humble dependence upon *him*, and renouncing all others, is really believing in *him*.

May the Lord bless thee and keep thee, be your leader, guide, and comfort. Kind love to your Niece, and all enquiring friends and acquaintance.—I must conclude this letter, with some Remarks I have met with on the very great difference between an *Acquaintance* and a *Friend*.

Your's truly,
Ruhamah.

ACQUAINTANCE and FRIENDS
DISTINCT CHARACTERS.

>FALLEN man an erring creature is,
>And, bent on erring, errs in this:
>He forms connections without end,
>And calls each *intimate a Friend*.

>But 'twixt the two a difference lies,
>And, oh! how great is our surprize—
>To view the characters more near,
>How vast me difference does appear.

>*Acquaintance* cries, to ease my woe,
>Be warm'd, be fill'd—and off they go.
>My *Friend* presents the thing I need,
>The *one's* in word, the *other* deed.

>While pleasing plenty crowns my cup,
>*Acquaintance* springs like mushrooms up;
>But woeful want creeps forth to light,
>And each betakes himself to flight.

>Yet sometimes one of human kind.
>In this dull day remains behind;
>And 'tis my *Friend*, for only he
>Cares for the child of misery.

>*Acquaintance* see me go astray:
>But he must look to that they say.
>My *Friend* seeks out my devious track,
>O'ertakes me, and conducts me back.

>If sick, or into prison thrown,
>My *Friend* still makes my case his own,
>And in my chamber or my cell
>Esteems it his delight to dwell.

The utmost my *Acquaintance* do,
While these great deeps I'm passing through,
Is, squeeze this prayer out now and then—
Heav'n send him safely out again.

Acquaintance are but sons of earth;
They relish well the house of mirth,
But in the mourner's dwelling place
'Tis real pain to shew his face.

Here mark my *Friend*, he in the hour
Of keen temptation's darkness power,
Stands by me all the season long,
With a sweet promise on his tongue.

He bears my company till death,
Whilst on my very latest breath;
And in his last kind act of love,
Points to my Father's house above.

Then while I sojourn here below,
Let *Friend* include all names I know;
And be it fellow-creature's pride
To know no other name beside.—*Amen.*

LETTER XI.

Valley of Achor, Feb. 25, 1819.

MY DEAR FRIEND, I. R. ESQ.

I am ashamed I have been so dilatory in answering your kind letter of the 10th instant. I read it with most exquisite delight. I intended a very long epistle for you, but I must still remain that in your debt, which I will faithfully pay the earliest opportunity. Yesterday I was just sitting down to drop you a line, but was suddenly surprized to hear of your indisposition. I fear your daily vexations have hurt your nervous system, and distressed your mind; nor have you much power to bear them—we all want strength to endure tribulation. We want power to stand in the evil day, that we may not fall before it. I have often been pleased, edified, and comforted with that very precious Promise, xliii. Isa. "When thou passest through the fire, thou shalt not be burned; when thou passest through the waters, they shall not overflow thee, for I am with thee." I trust this promise will be fulfilled in our experience *till* death, and *in* death. I feel anxious about your health of body. I judge your feelings. I know your state of mind. We need Divine keeping in every thing we do, and in every step we take. Hence, David prayed: Preserve me, O God, for in thee do I put my trust. Leave me not destitute. Does not this prayer suit you well? it does me. Yet I feel happy the Lord is leading you to see the vanity of all things below the stars; the emptiness of the creature, the sin of your nature, in hewing out cisterns, yea, broken cisterns, that can hold, retain, no water. No sooner are creature comforts in, but they run out again. Yet, alas, how awful for mankind to forsake the living fountain which never will be exhausted, or run dry! The adorable Trinity in unity, is that fountain, each glorious person is so represented, because they are equal in power, majesty, glory, and goodness. God is love, and this glorious Godhead includes the three Holy Ones. What a mercy for us, *they* divinely condescended to enter into covenant about us, such hell-deserving sinners as we are, and in the prospect of our miseries, made ample provision for us, that we might be infinite gainers by the fall, and God for ever glorified in that great business of redemption and grace.—In this glorious covenant our sins were made over to Christ, and his righteousness made over to us. This was secured by the promise, and the oath of God; confirmed by the blood of the dear Saviour; made known in the Gospel, and brought to the faith of an humble believer. After the sense and assurance of this blessing, we being first convinced of sin, and fearing God's wrath, the day of death, the last judgment and eternity, we doubt, fear, pray, hope, aspire, desire, long, and then grow careless, lukewarm, indifferent, dead, till guilt is felt again, or trouble arises, or affliction comes on; then we get alarmed, quickened, and anxious again to read our title clear, to see the interest Christ has in us, and the interest we have in *him*; to know that our sins are forgiven us, that God is at peace with us, that the law is magnified, sin put away, a door open in heaven that no sin in future can shut; death left stingless, judgment not at all dreaded, because we shall see *him* whom we *adore*, *admire*, and *love*; we shall be made like *him*, we shall get rid of sin.

> Sin, our worst enemy before,
> Shall vex our eyes and souls no more;
> But every power find sweet employ
> In Christ's eternal world of joy.

I beg the Lord, the Holy Spirit, to give you supernatural ideas of Christ, so as to endear *him* to your heart, and make you long to tell of *his name* and fame; to make you wise; to be as wise as Paul, and as eloquent as Apollos; that you might point forth the Divine excellencies of Jesus to poor sinners. I trust your life will be spared for this purpose, it is the only thing worth living for. Christ is the darling of the Father, and the grand object of the Spirit's glorification: angels adore *him*, saints admire *him*, and in our poor feeble way, oh that we could love *him* with every power and passion, with every member and faculty of body, soul and spirit. May this instrument of ten strings sweetly sound *his* dear fame. The most painful lesson we have to learn, is the evil of our hearts, the malice of the devil, the weakness of our own arm, and our utter impossibility to do any one good thing without Christ: separated from *him*, we can do nothing, no more than a dead branch can grow, that is cut off and thrown aside. The nature, extent, and spirituality of the law, and our condemnation by it, the person, the glory, and work of Christ, as the head of the church, and the Saviour of the body. This is the main subject, and the various displays of the offices of God, the Holy Spirit, as the glorifier of Christ. This subject is the Gospel itself, and the longer I live, the more blessed I see this truth. The Son of man is come to save that which was lost. This is an encouragement to my soul, and the very basis of my hope. Here alone is the way of access to God, to the Throne, and to Heaven. May the Spirit sanctify, and bless you; bear testimony with your spirit, that you are a child of God. This will be spiritual health in bodily sickness; this will light life in death, and gild the gloomy horrors of the tomb, as the celebrated Dr. Young says, and with which I conclude my epistle.

> Religion! thou the soul of happiness,
> And, groaning Calvary, of thee: there shine
> The noblest truths: there strongest motives sting:
> There sacred violence assaults the soul;
> There nothing but compulsion is forborne.
> Can love allure us? or can terror awe?
> He weeps!—the falling drop puts out the sun.
> He sigh!—the sigh earth's deep foundation shakes.

> If in *his* love so terrible, what then
> *His* wrath inflam'd? *His* tenderness on fire?
> Like soft, smooth oil, out-blazing other fires?

Pray do let me know how you are in health as soon as you can.—Kind love to Mrs. R. wishing you a healthy body and a prosperous soul.

I remain,

Dear friend,
Your's truly,
Ruhamah.

LETTER XII.

Valley of Achor, March 16, 1819.

To I. R. Esq.

MY DEAR SIR,

I am truly happy to hear that the Lord has restored you again in some measure to health. I was much affected at the news of your sudden indisposition, and knew not what was the will of God concerning you, but through mercy, I trust your spared life is for the glory of God, and will be a means of your increasing in knowledge, that your mind may be better prepared for the special Service of God, and that you may be ready to take your flight as soon as the *Lord*, the *Master* cometh and calleth for you. Every attack of the constitution is a messenger sent to let us know our frailty: these tabernacles of flesh are but weak, and hang on a precarious thread; our bones are the *stakes*, the *cords* are the sinews, and the *breath* is the main pillar. Great God, on what a slender thread hangs everlasting things; the eternal state of all the dead hangs on such feeble strings.

God has laid an everlasting foundation for *his* dear people in the everlasting covenant; the effect of *his* everlasting love, the profound depth of *his* infinite wisdom, which has secured an everlasting salvation, by an everlasting righteousness, which will be to the everlasting praise of Jehovah, and to the everlasting joy of *his* dear church.

> Then at *his* throne our crowns we'll cast,
> And shout, I am saved, I am saved at last!

Your indisposition, and indeed every other calamity is as that messenger of whom the prophet Elisha gave orders to notice, Look, as when the messenger cometh, hold him fast, and shut to the door, is not the sound of his master's feet behind? So may we detain every message of sorrow. Ask the question, Why is this sent me? what does he say from his master? But why ask this? the sound of Christ is heard, Behold, I come quickly. Our deep concern of soul, and every conviction of sin, every fear of death, judgment, and eternity should be entertained, thought over, and made use of, to go to God with, and entreat the manifestation of pardoning love and mercy. Hence, *he* has promised to be found of them that seek *him*, to be found as a God in Christ, in whom all fulness dwells, and having all the blessings of an everlasting covenant to bestow upon the heirs of promise. *He* giveth to them just as they need; but these blessings are only given to the poor and helpless, the lost, the guilty, and the vile, and till this is the case with us, we can never be in earnest about Christ, and *his* Salvation. Wretches that feel what help they need, will bless the helping hand; and till the Saviour puts forth *his* power, we can do no more than the mariners did with Jonah aboard; the men rowed hard to bring it to land, but the sea wrought, and was tempestuous against them. Christ is the only one who can still the tempest of a distressed mind, and bring us on our knees, exclaiming, What manner of *man* is this, that even the winds and sea obey *him*. This is a comfort to me in my most dreary prospects.

I remain yours,
With respect,
Ruhamah.

LETTER XIII.

London, September 10, 1820.

MY MUCH BELOVED FRIEND, I. R. ESQ.

Mrs. P. did me the honor to call on me last night with the very painful news of the departure of your dear John. A variety of serious ideas flowed into my mind upon hearing of your affecting and serious loss. I knew how much you loved him, how dear he was to you both; I knew how very engaging he had become; I considered your feelings on the occasion, nor was I without my fears, lest you should reflect on yourselves in taking him so long a journey. I have also pictured to myself your absence from the little pious society of friends amongst us, your large and venerable house. Recent death of an aged parent, with none but strangers around you, and a variety of circumstances beside; these, yes, these things dwell on my mind, and have led me to trouble you with a line on the sad occasion. I hope an apology for intrusion is needless. I write not to *inform* my beloved friends, but only to *remind* them, that every event is absolutely decreed by a God of infinite wisdom; not a stroke of affliction, nor a shaft of death can possibly touch, but by Divine appointment. The *nature*, the *kind*, the *time*, the *age*, the *place* were all arranged in the unerring purposes of God. It was decreed the dear dear boy should be taken to B. Hall, *there* the Lord would send for him. He has sent for his own: the Lord had the greatest right to him, he was, indeed, lent to his affectionate parents, but he is demanded back again; he was the object of his heavenly father's love, he was the property of Jesus, and he must be brought home to his house, by his holy angels. Death indeed is very terrible to our natures, it takes away the darlings of our hearts, and the desire of our eyes, but it has transmitted yours to the enjoyment of God in human nature: this is the accomplishment of God's design in this providence, and with holy joy you will one day say, *He* has done all things well. The dear boy, like Abraham in his conversion, has left his native country, and gone into the eternal inheritance, which God has prepared for him, and which he never saw or sought before. Like Jacob, he at the command of his God, has returned to his father's house, and his own spiritual and angelic kindred: like the Israelites, though his journey was short, God opened a passage through the garden of death: his little journey is ended, he sets in peace, *it is well*. Farewell, my dear-little fellow, I shall kiss thy little lips or press thy little cheeks no more! no, no, the painful task is assigned to thy dear parents, to see thee taken from their arms, and from their house, to the solemn tomb, the silent, the dark, the cold, the dreary receptacle for suffering mortality. Happy voyager, how short thy passage on the sea of this tribulated world; how short thy stay, how swift thy flight; but what thy surprize to enter into another state of love, holiness, joy, and glory; every little power expanded, and the soul plunged in a moment into a sea of bliss: what a glorious transition, what a surprize, and perhaps the first object it saw, was its little sister at the portals of bliss, waiting to welcome him home, although unknown before, yet now known to each other for ever. Methinks I see them meet and clasp each other with holy innocent joy, and if a thought could be indulged, or received about their beloved parents: surely they converse together about you: but hark, they speak to you! they bid you weep not; (if ye loved us ye would rejoice we are gone to our Father, and the world seeth us no more. Hallelujah.)

I hope dear Mrs. R. will be most divinely supported under this bereavement. I trust the dear little one in London will be restored to be a comfort, but dear John is this moment fresh in my mind. I judge your feelings; I am sorry you are so far distant from us. I have the departure of my own beloved daughter still in mind, the thought often occurs: well, let us look up, let us take courage, we shall bless God for their loss another day; we are left to endure many a conflict, many a trial, many a grief, but the soft hand of Jesus has wiped off the tears from his little face: it is ours to suffer toil and grief, till death transmits us, burdened and tired, grieved, and tried, to that glory which never fades away; it is well for us that the dear Redeemer has been through the territories of death and the grave, that he has taken the sting of the one, and overcome the other for us. May his love solace your mind; may his grace reign in your hearts; may his power protect you, and his very gracious presence cheer your souls; the separation is painful, but it is short. Our days fly swiftly away, the night of death will come on; it may not be very distant, but interested in Jesus, pardoned and justified, influenced, and led by his spirit, we shall meet in a brighter, and better abode.

God bless you both together with his supporting hand. So prays your sympathizing friend, and best wisher in Christ.

Ruhamah.

LETTER XIV.

Valley of Achor, August 13, 1819.

MY DEAR FRIEND, MRS. M.

I trust you are as well in mind and body as you expect to be in a time state. I have cause to bless God for all I have experienced, even for the bitter path of sorrow. But I have had much of the Lord's goodness pass before me, and *he* has manifested his dear name to me, as the Lord, the Lord God, gracious and merciful, abundant in goodness, in mercy, and truth; and though *he* can by no means (of a sinner's devising) clear the guilty, yet *he* has devised a plan, in infinite wisdom, whereby *he* can be just, and yet the justifier of the ungodly. And it is our mercy that we are brought from all confidence in the flesh, while a daily acquaintance with the depravity of our hearts, keeps us from trusting in self; the troubles of life keep us from making up our happiness in the world, and the hypocrisy of professors, with the weakness of God's *own* children, keeps us from looking to, and idolizing the creature; thus we tread the same path which the pious prophet Micah did, when he wrote his seventh chapter, and came to this blessed conclusion, *Therefore* will I look to the Lord: this is all that the blessed spirit aims at in bringing us low in soul, in the church, and in the world. My time flies fast; I dread to enter into the field of battle again. I am weaker in myself than ever I was, but perhaps the power of Christ will the more sensibly rest upon me. I hope to return with the olive branch of peace, while our adorable Noah opens the window, and puts forth his hand to receive me into the ark. I should like to come to the Lord's family loaded; I know they are a needy people, and the Lord has provided many things for them: *he* keeps a good table, though the family have not always an appetite to enjoy the rich provisions of his house; but the ever-kind householder has provisions suited to every one. I hope, therefore, to bring with me a little of the sincere milk of the word, for the children, that they may grow thereby, and some solid meat for those who are strong: the fatted calf, the roasted paschal lamb, without a bitten herb; an olive berry, from the uppermost bough; three loaves, also some unleavened bread, and a cake, baked under the tree. Some butter and neat honey from the rock, with the honey comb. Some broiled fish, also out of the sea of Tiberias; and as we may want a desert also, I hope to bring some apples, some nuts, and almonds; a bunch of figs, to take inwardly, or to make a plaister of, to lay on some sore place. Some good grapes of Eshcol, and pomegranates, and mandrakes; also a bottle of new wine, well refined. Some rock water, clear as chrystal, from the well of Bethlehem; this will be very cheering to some of the family. I hope also to bring some very beautiful flowers; a lovely *rose*, without a thorn; a remarkable *lily*, in full bloom, which grows in certain vallies, and many other lovely flowers; some only in bud, and some in full blossom: but I have not mentioned one-half the good things in our master's house. Let these suffice at present. I only want ability to get things ready, and then to call the guests, and to deliver out the various portions, as they are designed: but what do you think? though I am such a poor servitor, yet my master takes the trouble to teach me himself, and I never get scolded, without I act wrong, and am always forgiven, though I am often shut up in the coal cellar, yet not half so often as I deserve. About three years ago I sadly neglected the kitchen, and the setting out the table: I grew very careless, soiled my livery, and mingled even with the very enemies of my master; this was very ungrateful. I lost my place by it, and have been out of place this two years, yet my master is very kind to me; *he* keeps me all the time I am out of place, often sends to me, and has been several times to see me. He has forgiven my folly, and I expect to be hired again, about the ninth hour of the day, and then I shall bring all the things I have mentioned, and a good many things more. I expect a double honor upon me, for I hope to be steward also, as well as cook and butler, for you must know we have a charming wardrobe, and every one of his Benjamins are to have five changes of raiment; some are to be worn every day, but others only on court days, and public days. The outer one is to be always kept white, and though bad fellows throw dirt on it, yet we must not do so ourselves. What they throw on us will not stick, but what we do, is sure to abide; this is very remarkable. But I had almost forgot the music, a high sounding organ, a harp of ten strings, a cymbal, a lute, a violin, a tabret, and some silver trumpets, as a dance is expected, xxxi. Jeremiah, ver. 4.—We have also got in my master's house, some armour shoes, which look very beautiful, and fit every ones feet in the family, and they are so strong, that they are like iron and brass; there is a two-edged sword, a battle-axe, a helmet, a shield, a breast plate, and a bow with many precious arrows: thus you see how well we are provided, and in order to pass away our time pleasantly, and for our comfort and instruction, we have a good collection of books; histories, records, and ancient settlements, and a will or testament: and will you believe it? I think *your* name is in it. I have not time to tell you about the ornaments, with the dresses, but there are ear-rings, nose jewels, necklaces, bracelets, and all powders of the merchant, and as to money, it has all the king's stamp upon it. Some have but little, but others are well stored with it; and there is but one piece that is ever lost, and when one of the family has once had it, and lost it, a light is brought, the house is swept, and no rest felt till it is found again. May my dear friends be thus entertained in the banqueting house, while the banner of love is displayed over their heads.

Grace be with you all.—Kind respects to your family.

Your's,
Ruhamah.

I once read an excellent letter on this subject, in the Gospel Magazine. I wish you could procure it for me; it was written many years ago.

LETTER XV.

Valley of Achor, May 2, 1819.

MY DEAR MRS. F.

My heart feels truly grateful, that you remember me in my low estate. There are thousands in a profession, who boast much of their morality, and good works, and who may boast in the last day, that they have done many wonderful works; but God lays this to their charge, they are not grieved for the afflictions of Joseph! Such hypocrites are generally the most godly, where there are the most lookers on. My deep tribulations have tried many, and they have fled in the day of evil. What would such persons do, should persecution ever visit our land; and when it becomes a disgrace to profess religion? Nothing but the love of Christ in the heart, and that love kept up, and manifested under the sacred power of the holy Spirit, can enable a person to go on in the midst of opposition, or in the summer of prosperity; for it is a well known truth, that trials have slain their thousands, but prosperity its ten thousands. I well know *now*, what these words mean, "It is my happiness below, not to live without the cross:" this cross galls the old man of sin, but it is the means of the spiritual growth of the new man. Hence, the afflicted king once said, Lord, by these things men live, and in all these things is the life of my spirit. Faith, if genuine has something to do in the furnace; but when all is calm, she is inactive, and dull; hope is languid, and love is not seen. I feel assured in my own, my *right* mind, that this event *will* be for the glory of God, and for much good to me, and to many: but enemies will no doubt, always triumph, and say, Ah! there, so we would have it! yet their joy is but as the crackling of thorns, under a pot; it will not last long; only a blaze and a noise, and then it will evaporate, like smoke. I hope I shall love God for this rod, as well as for every other blessing. I never fully understood the Psalmist till I came here, when he said, Thy rod, and thy staff, they comfort me. Solomon explains it thus; To the hungry soul every bitter thing is sweet, because this rod is as much an evidence of our adoption, as any promise can be. They shall all pass under the rod, and they will say at last, our Jesus has done all things well. Ezekiel and John were to eat a book; this was sweet in the mouth, but bitter in the belly. So it is the case with us; the promise of fatherly correction is sweet to faith, but bitter to the old man of sin. Nature flinches, but grace strengthens the mind; bows the will, and resigns the soul to the will of God. *His* will and our wills are then in sweet unison; we are agreed, and though we sigh, yet rebellion is kept under, by all conquering grace; as a good woman once said, Though I groan I do not grumble, yet she was sorely afflicted.

> But, why should I complain, of want, or distress;
> Affliction or pain, *he* told me no less.

It is our mercy, the Saviour has borne the curse, and of course took it out of all our sorrows; we have the cup of tribulation, but the curse is gone; Jesus has taken it away, and neither sin nor Satan, the world, or man can bring it back. This was done by the great act of the Saviour's sorrows, when *he* entered the garden of Gethsemane, and agonized there, when the sorrows of his sacred soul were past all description; and when he cried out on the cross, It is finished! Yes, our dear Lord knew then the work was done, in his putting away sin. *He* felt it was done, in his soul, as *his* God and Father shone again, as well as the sun did at three o'clock the afternoon of his death: it was *after* noon, indeed; the burning sun of God's Wrath laid hot upon *him*, till justice was satisfied, and then the indignation ceased for ever. This was *afternoon*. I drop this hint only, but oh, that our minds were more affected with his *sorrows* than they are. Think *of these two lines:*

> Canst thou, ungrateful man, his torments *see?*
> Nor shed one tear for him who shed his blood for *thee?*

I pray God to grant my dear friend very sweet views of her dear Lord, on the work *he* has accomplished. May the holy Spirit visit you, and shine upon your spirit, and help you to believe in Jesus, and so to find *him* precious, that you may know your sins are forgiven you.

Very kind respects to mother; to brother James, your companion, and my friend.

Your's truly,
Ruhamah.

LETTER XVI.

Valley of Achor, March 26, 1818.

MY DEAR FRIEND, MISS D.,

What apology shall I make for my long delay, but lowness of mind, and a tedious winter; and this, *with* you, I am sure is quite apology enough. I write you, concerning the once crucified, but now exalted *Jesus*. As it is the wish of my soul, to live to fill up the cup of some poor believer's consolation, though I am denied that privilege at present, yet I hope to throw a mite into the Gospel treasury for you, by sending a few imperfect lines, which I must beg you to accept. O that I had but *the* wisdom of Solomon, *the* piety of a David, *the* knowledge of a Paul, *the* fervour of an Isaiah, *the* faith of an Abraham, *the* love of a John, with *the* tearful affections of a Mary, that I might speak good of his name. *Christ* is all in all; *he* is the very glory in the centre of Heaven, as the sun is in the universe. *He* is the joy of Heaven; and though *he* is far off us, yet *he* has promised ever to be with us. *He* is exactly suited to us in all our wants, and the love of Jehovah is in no case so eminently displayed, as in providing such a *Jesus* for us. So great, so kind, so glorious, and yet so precious. We shall soon be done time, and commence upon an eternal scene; then our knowledge will be complete, though no doubt, it will be expanding for ever, and the effects of it, even in Heaven, will be wonder, humility, and love, for the mind will incessantly be employed in roving over the glories of God; as the God of all grace, one in three, and three in one; seen, apprehended, enjoyed, beheld, and loved in *Christ Jesus*.

> And now they range the heavenly plains,
> And sing *his* love in melting strains;
> Or, overwhelm'd with rapture sweet,
> Sink down, adoring at *his* feet.

May this be our lot, and in order to that *state*, that *bliss*, that *joy*, and that sweet *employment*. May the eternal spirit give us such views of Christ, as shall cause us to long for the time.

We are poor sinners, guilty, and hell-deserving, condemned by a holy law, and exposed to a thousand miseries in this world; and in our fallen nature, to the woe of perdition. Christ is the Saviour of the lost; *he* was from all eternity raised up, and voluntarily offered *himself* to become the Saviour of *his* church. Say ye of *him*, whom the Father hath sanctified—and for their sakes I sanctify *myself*. Set apart, separated, for *his* peoples' salvation. Glory be to *his* dear name: *he* is God and man; had *he* been only God, we could not have been saved; had *he* been man only, *he* would not have been able to save us; but *he* is God and man; this at once secures the honors of *his* law, the glory of *his* perfections, and the salvation of *his* church. As God and man, *he* is the Lord, our righteousness, and as the atonement, which alone is efficacious, *he* is called the Lord and God, who laid down *his* life, and purchased the church with *his* blood. How most divinely adapted *he* was, and *is*, to save us. What a glorious meeting of divine excellencies are in *him*. Hence, the Father calls upon us, to behold *him*, Behold my servant, whom I uphold. The Lord Jesus declares, *he* will say of *himself*, Behold me, behold me! to a people who had not known *him*! and the holy Spirit points *him* out, by John; Behold the Lamb of God! I know my dear friend desires to know *him*, that she may believe in *him*, and love *him*. This encourages me to go on with my sweet subject, which I hope will not prove tedious to you. The person of Christ is most wonderful, it is greater than *his* glorious works, and ought to be for ever the theme of our discourse. Permit me, then, just to observe, there meets in Jesus, infinite *highness*, and infinite *humility*—infinite *glory*, and infinite *condescension*—infinite *grace*, and infinite *justice*—infinite *majesty*, and transcendent *meekness*—the deepest *reverence* of God, and an *equality* with God—infinite *worthiness* of good, and the greatest *patience* under evils—wonderful *obedience*, and supreme *dominion* over heaven and earth—the most perfect *resignation*, and absolute *sovereignty*—an entire *trust* in God, and yet *self sufficiency* in *himself*. *Justice*, *mercy*, and *truth* are sweetly combined in *him*, displayed through *him*, and shines in all *he* says, and in all *he* does; while, as an high priest, *he* makes intercession—as God and man, *he* demands the very blessings: Father, I will, that those whom thou hast given *me*, be with *me*. He is the *lion* to our foes; the *lamb* to our faith, and at times, *he* appears the *lion* in providence, while *he* is the lamb, in a way of grace, to the soul. This is your *Christ*.

> All over glorious, is our Lord,
> To be admired, and yet ador'd:
> *His* worth, if all the nations knew,
> I'm sure the world would love *him* too.

And so says,
Your's truly,
Ruhamah.

LETTER XVII.

Valley of Achor, March 25, 1818.

MY KIND FRIEND, MRS. O.

Grace and peace be to you. The wise and good, but solemn providence of God, having deprived me of the public opportunity of comforting my afflicted friends, I have no other means of doing it, but by a few lines, about the best, the most import, and precious objects, which will take eternity itself, fully to unfold. You, doubtless, must lament with me, the narrowness of our minds, in receiving the most blessed things, with *the* intrusion of necessary business—*the* cares of life—*the* heavy conflicts we have also to experience, with many painful visits from the enemy of our souls—*the* native reluctant of the body, and *the* pressure of many trying thoughts. *These* hinder our running the heavenly race, *these* keep us down, so that we cannot rise in heavenly mindedness; and a sense of our past sins, makes us ready to halt, so that we cannot walk comfortably. But though this is our case, yet blessed be God, we are not in despair, nor are we out of the promise: They that wait on the Lord, shall renew their strength; and blessed are all they that wait for me. This made David deliver this charge: *My soul, wait thou only on God, for my expectation is from him.* What, alas! should we do without the promises? Grace made them, but the hand of divine truth is to make them good. Our wants, woes, and miseries, were all known and consulted, by the adorable trinity; and dark as we are about the mystery of God, all is clear to himself. But I lament, I feel a proneness to judge of the Lord, by carnal reason, and this is like judging of an unfinished picture, by the original. We must stay till it is finished: or, like judging of a watch, when it is all in pieces; we may admire it when put together. I often catch myself at this work, especially when I am very low, nervous, and tried in mind, temper, and providence. This is very carnal. May the blessed spirit quicken faith to rise, and wing its way to eternal love, eternal grace, eternal mercy, and eternal kindness. This is its proper element: here we are at home; here is liberty, peace, joy, and satisfaction. Here we see infinite wisdom, contriving a *time* when, a *place* where, and a *manner* how merciful kindness, and melting pity should be manifested. Here we see every sweet attribute harmonize, and every grace displayed, while the cross of your dear lovely, loving Saviour appears truly glorious. See the cluster of excellencies around it, hymning its praises, with harps of love. *Faith* begins the song; *hope*, full of immortality joins; *loves* notes are clearly heard; *joy* is sweetly provoked to help repentance with her deep sounding notes. *Zeal* most cheerfully moves her fingers on the harp, while *fear*, more silently, more reverently touches the strings. *Patience* most meekly assists, and *humility* sounds her simple airs; yet there is not one discordant string. Angels listen, and the redeemed above, beckon us home to the general assembly, that all may bear in the chorus. And this will be the burden of the song; worthy is the lamb that was slain: but why the Lamb? but because, in *him*, and in *his* love, person and work, all the glory of the God of grace is most eminently displayed.

> Here we see the Father's *grace*,
> Beaming in the Saviour's *face*.

In Christ Jesus the glory of God shines, and God is glorified in *him*; and God glorified Christ, as man-mediator in himself, when *he* brought *him* from the dead, and set *him* at *his* own right hand. Gave *him* to be head over all things, and to fill *his* people with spiritual good. *He* was deeply humbled, and sorely tried—*he* was sharply tempted, and sadly afflicted, before *his* exaltation, and we must be conformed to *his* image. Before honor, is humility. Christ found it so, and all *his* followers must. But when troubles abound, is it not strange? that though this is the very time the Saviour is most *tender*, most *careful*, and most *indulgent* of us, as a parent is of a sick child, more than the strong and healthy. Yet these are the very seasons we have most fears, most cares, and most terrors; when, in reality, we have the least reason. How then, is that text? For my thoughts are not as your thoughts, nor my ways as your ways, saith the Lord. And it is very remarkable, that the greatest part of the precious promises are made to the tried people of God. I pray the God of all grace, to strengthen our faith in *his* love, in *his* grace, in *his* truth, and in *his* word. O that when we open the Bible, we could always think we are opening, and looking into the very heart of God *himself*, as a God of love; but we are too apt to read for others, and say, O what sweet things are here for God's children. Yes, they are for us, and whatever suits us, that is ours. Whatsoever things were written afore time, were written for us, that *we* might have strong consolation, who have fled for refuge, and we have fled; trouble, guilt, sin, fear, Satan, world, and conscience has pursued; but as faith gathers strength in the person, and work of Christ, we find they cannot hurt us. Thy vengeance will not strike us *here*; nor Satan dares our souls invade. Frighten us he may, but reign, *he* never can any more. No, our hearts are bespoke. Christ is the lover, and faith, prayer, desire, and intreaty has said most sincerely, Take my poor heart! Set me as a seal upon thine heart. Lord, take and make me thine! take me as I am. Amen.

Your's truly,
Ruhamah.

LETTER XVIII.

Valley of Achor, July 26, 1819.

MY DEAR FRIEND, MRS. R.

I am exceedingly grieved to hear of your indisposition of body. This is the reason, no doubt, why I have not seen you for so long a time: but in a few months more, I hope to see you at Mount Gilead.

> I soon shall get from Achor's Vale,
>   To Gilead's Mount remove;
> And ever tell, the untold tale,
>   Of everlasting love.

There is balmy consolation in Gilead, amongst the *heap* of *witnesses*, and a real physician *there*, to heal every wound that sin has made. I long to be at that mount. But many, alas! surround it, that never feed on it—many walk about Zion, that never enter into it, and many have the word, and desire the word, that never did desire, or enjoy the sincere *milk* of it. You and I know that there can be no feeding without life, and this life is seen by the appetite. Blessed are they, that hunger and thirst after righteousness; after an increasing knowledge of *it*, and after a divine enjoyment of *it*—to be found in *it*, in death, and to be owned in *it*, in the last great day. Ah! this is the rich robe. I pray my dear friend may be found adorned with it, when the judge shall appear in awful grandeur; when the elements shall melt with fervent heat; when the stars shall fall from their sockets, and when sun and moon; when the grand planetary orbs shall be thrown into promiscuous ruin, and all creation fly away before the face of *him*, who will ere long swear, that time shall be no more. There are two precious promises, confirmed by the path of a covenant God. *He* swore by himself, that in blessing, *he* would bless *his* people. *He* has sworn *he* never will be wroth with, nor rebuke *his* people. This is sweet food for precious faith. O may you feast on it divinely. Because *he* could swear by no greater, *He* swore by himself, saying, I declare, in blessing you, I will bless you. Eternal life is in God's blessing, and this life being in Christ, in blessing, God blesses us for evermore.—I trust my dear friend's mind is often led to the Saviour, and that you prove *his* preciousness in *his* sacred person, *his* covenant love, *his* meritorious obedience, and *his* atoning blood—*his* prevalent intercession, and *his* advocacy with the Father. This is the glorious object of faith, and round *him* faith hovers, till it can gather strength enough to lay hold of *him*—to *him* it often looks, and always bends; and close to *him* it cleaves, as the fond ivy entwines round the oak. This, you doubtless, see in your lowest state, even when low in body, weak in nerves, barren in mind, tried in the world, and grieved in the church; and when nature is reluctant; the flesh a heavy clog, and the spirits within, seem to sink into earth, as its centre. Yet there is a going to our spiritual David, though in as helpless a state as lame Mephibosheth, or aged Barzillai. I have had many strange changes of mind since I last saw you, but I was never more sensible of the carrying on, and increase of the work of God in my soul, than I am now. In my very best state, I can never rise above this motto. *Full of the deepest need.* And this line following, expresses the warmest desires of my heart. Thou, oh Christ, art all I want. I am learning, daily, to know *his* value. I feel my need of *him* increases, and strange to tell, the lower I sink in this frame, the higher I rise in confidence—in a confidence that I never did so fully attain before; for if I had a little of it in times past, company, visiting, the neglect of prayer, and carelessness of manners, lamed me in both feet. But I find it most blessed to be kept near the Saviour. I have had some blessed views of *him*, and I am covetous for more. I want to enjoy *his* love, and to walk in *him*—to be adorned with *his* light—to be crowned with *his* loving kindness—to rise superior to the world—to fight the good fight, and so to lay hold on eternal life—to apprehend, embrace, and enjoy the everlasting favours of God.

I hope my good friend, Mr. R. is well in health and spirits, as trying times, and body of sin and death will permit. I hope he is growing in knowledge. This will increase faith, and beget a blessed confidence, that maketh not ashamed. The main point with us, is, to beg the Lord, the holy Spirit, to create a supernatural faculty in our minds, to take in subjects, truly supernatural, that our affections may be supernatural also; and where this is the privilege, the mercy and the honor, it is a most divine evidence, that our persons are in Christ. The most blessed subject we can ever apprehend, is the love of God. O to be led with some power to this, so as to conceive of it, as set upon us. What a favour! We often judge of it by its effects upon us, and by reflecting on what the holy Spirit has wrought in us. This is a good plan sometimes; but are there not periods in your experience, when you doubt of the reality of the Spirit's work on your own heart? I find it the most blessed method in my very worst, and in my very best frame, to fall low at the feet of Jesus, and to study the love of God, to guilty man, with the joint operation of each adorable person in the trinity, on the heart. The Father convinces, chastens, and teaches us, out of *his* law, and testifies of *his* dear son to us. *He* then brings us to Christ; the son accepts us, pardons, justifies, receives, and owns us as *his* own, while the Holy Spirit, acts as a divine comforter, sealer, and witness. And when this is experienced, we have the witness of the water, the blood, and the spirit; and these three agree in one, to witness our adoption, and the love of God to us, in Christ Jesus. This, and this only, reconciles the mind to bear the cross, daily, whether it be reproach or bondage, whether it be weakness of body, or trying circumstances, or even if they all come together.

Duties, and trials then appear;
Easy to do, or light to bear.
Whether they many be, or few,
We, through *this* strength, can all things do.

I remain,

Your's truly,
Ruhamah.

www.ingramcontent.com/pod-product-compliance
Ingram Content Group UK Ltd.
Pitfield, Milton Keynes, MK11 3LW, UK
UKHW042152281224
453045UK00004B/351